FARMERS AND RANCHERS

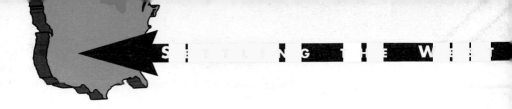

FARMERS AND RANCHERS

BRETT HARVEY

TWENTY–FIRST CENTURY BOOKS

A Division of Henry Holt and Company
New York

Twenty-First Century Books
A Division of Henry Holt and Company, Inc.
115 West 18th Street
New York, NY 10011

Henry Holt ® and colophon are trademarks of
Henry Holt and Company, Inc.
Publishers since 1866

Library of Congress Cataloging-in-Publication Data
Harvey, Brett.
Farmers and ranchers / Brett Harvey. — 1st ed.
p. cm. — (Settling the West)
Includes bibliographical references (p.   ) and index.
1. West (U.S.)—History—Juvenile literature. 2. West (U.S.)—Description and travel. 3.
Frontier and pioneer life—West (U.S.)—Juvenile literature. 4. Ranchers—West (U.S.)—
History—19th century—Juvenile literature. 5. Farmers—West (U.S.)—History—19th
century—Juvenile literature. I. Title. II. Series.
F591.H273 1995

978'.02—dc20   94–39904
                                                               CIP
                                                                AC

ISBN 0–8050–2999–0
First Edition 1995

Cover design by Kelly Soong
Interior design by Helene Berinsky

Printed in the United States of America
All first editions are printed on acid-free paper∞
10 9 8 7 6 5 4 3 2 1

Photo Credits

p. 2: Stephen Studd / Tony Stone Worldwide; pp. 16, 17, 21, 24, 31, 37, 43, 44, 51, 53, 57,
63, 64, 67, 70, 74, 80: North Wind Picture Archives; p. 20: Oregon Historical
Society / OrHi 91218; p. 29: Charles Haire; p. 35: D. Kinsey Collection / Whatcom
Museum of History and Art, Bellingham, Wash.; p. 39: Washington State Historical
Society, Tacoma, Wash.; p. 47: UPI / Bettmann; p. 72 (both): City of Greeley Museums,
Permanent Collection; p. 81: Colorado Historical Society.

EDITOR'S NOTE

A great deal of research went into finding interesting first-person accounts that would give the reader a vivid picture of life on the western frontier. In order to retain the "flavor" of these accounts, original spelling and punctuation have been kept in most instances.

History told in the words of men and women who lived at the time lets us become a part of their lives . . . lives of ordinary people who met extraordinary challenges to settle the West.

—P.C.

CONTENTS

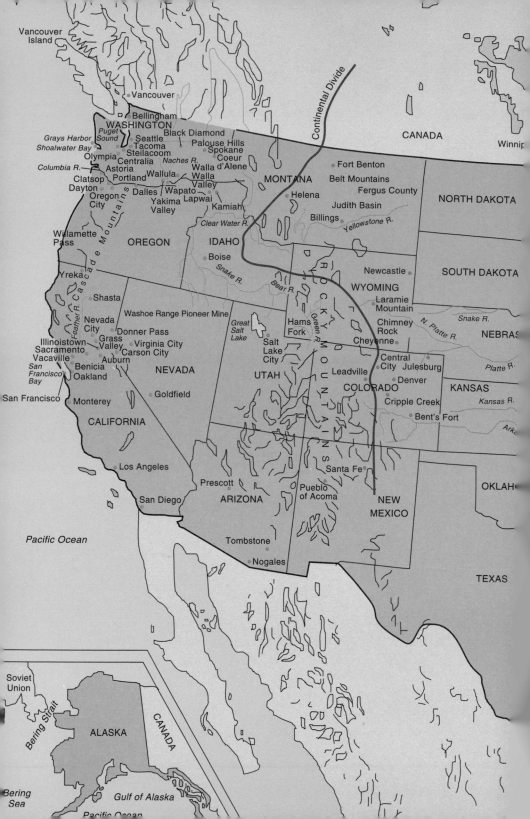

SETTLING THE WEST
Many of the places mentioned in the series are located on this map.

NESOTA

MICHIGAN

WISCONSIN

WA

Dubuque

ncil Bluffs

ha

t. Joseph

Nauvoo

ssouri R.

St. Louis

dependence

MISSOURI

ARKANSAS

ILLINOIS

INDIANA

OHIO

KENTUCKY

TENNESSEE

MISSISSIPPI

ALABAMA

LOUISIANA

WEST VIRGINIA

VIRGINIA

NORTH CAROLINA

SOUTH CAROLINA

GEORGIA

FLORIDA

MAINE

VT

NH

Lowell

NEW YORK

Seneca Falls

Boston

MA

Taunton

CT

RI

Plainfield

PENNSYLVANIA

New York City

Philadelphia

Baltimore

NJ

MARYLAND

WASHINGTON

Atlantic Ocean

Gulf of Mexico

CUBA

MAJOR TRAILS TO THE WEST

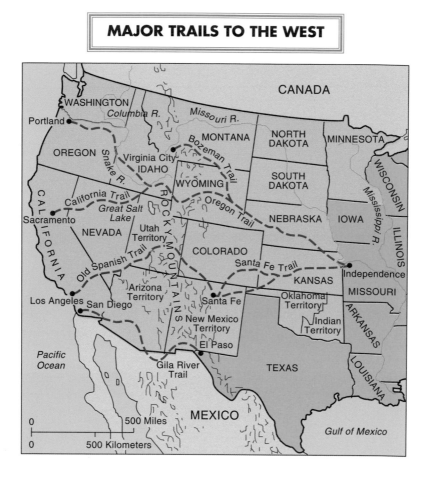

INTRODUCTION

From 1840 to 1870 an astonishing event took place in America: a quarter of a million people uprooted themselves and migrated westward across the continent. They were headed for something called "the frontier"—the place where the civilized world of houses and towns and schools and shops ended and the wilderness began. From Maine to Kansas, whole families as well as individual men and women sold their possessions, piled into covered wagons, and began the long trek west. They weren't sure how to get there and they weren't sure what they'd find when they arrived. They left behind their homes, their relatives, their friends, and everything safe and familiar to go on this terrifying adventure.

Today, we can fly from Illinois to California in a few hours. In the 1800s, traveling by covered wagon, the trip could take six to eight months full of hardship and danger. Why in the world did they go? Some went because they hoped to find gold, some went as missionaries, some went to start businesses. But most of the people who went west were farming families from the Midwest, where the soil was worn out. They were lured by the promise of finding free land, better soil to grow their crops on, and an easier life.

1

LEAVING HOME

In 1842, the U.S. Congress passed a law protecting farmers who improved their land. "Come along, come along—don't be alarmed, Uncle Sam is rich enough to give us all a farm," went a popular camp song of the day.[1] That was enough to persuade Phoebe Judson, who set out for the West with her family from Vermillion, Ohio, in 1853:

"The motive that induced us to part with the pleasant associations and the dear friends of our childhood days was to obtain from the government of the United States a grant of land that 'Uncle Sam' had promised to give to the head of each family that settled in this new country. This, we hoped, would make us independent, for as yet we did not possess a home of our own."[2]

The few adventurers who had actually made the trip west in the 1830s brought back amazing tales that dazzled the ears of all who heard them. One farmer's son told how his family heard about Oregon:

"One Saturday morning father said that he was going

to hear Mr. Burnett talk about Oregon. . . . Mr. Burnett hauled a box out on to the sidewalk, took his stand upon it, and began to tell us about the land flowing with milk and honey on the shores of the Pacific. . . . He told of the great crops of wheat which it was possible to raise in Oregon, and pictured in glowing terms the richness of the soil and the attractions of the climate, and then with a little twinkle in his eye he said 'and they do say, gentlemen, they do say, that out in Oregon the pigs are running about under the great acorn trees, round and fat, and already cooked, with knives and forks sticking in them so that you can cut off a slice whenever you are hungry.' . . . Father was so moved by what he heard that he decided to join the company that was going west to Oregon."[3]

Not everyone was so eager to go on this great adventure. In most families, the decision to go west was made by the man. Many women were frightened of the journey and reluctant to leave their families because they believed they would never see them again. But in those days, a wife usually did what her husband told her. "Dr. Wilson has determined to go to California. I am going with him, as there is no alternative," Margaret Wilson wrote to her mother in 1850.[4]

But some women, especially if they were young and had no children yet, were as excited about going west as their husbands. Miriam Thompson Tuller was eighteen and newly married when she and her husband set out for Oregon in 1845. "I was possessed with a spirit of adventure and a desire to see what was new and strange," she later recalled.[5]

Although very few unmarried women went in these caravans, at least one, a young woman named Elizabeth

Wood, went for the sheer adventure of it: "I have a great desire to see Oregon," she explained. "The beautiful scenery of plain and mountains and . . . the wild animals and the Indians, and natural curiosities in abundance."[6]

When the time came to leave home, a crowd of family and friends gathered to say good-bye. It was a time of great sadness, but four-year-old Marianne Hunsaker was too little to be anything but excited.

"Two of my earliest recollections are of asking Father what Oregon was. Everyone seemed to be talking of it. Father said, 'It is a place. We are going there. It is in that direction,' and he pointed toward the fireplace, which happened to be toward the west. . . . My next vivid recollection was of having our relatives, friends, and neighbors gather at our place, and as we drove westward they waved their hands and said, 'Farewell, farewell.' Most of the women began to cry, saying, 'We shall never see you again.' I wondered what that word 'farewell' meant, so finally I asked Mother, and she told me it was a more stylish way of saying goodbye."[7]

Virginia Reed, who was thirteen when her family left Springfield, Illinois, was old enough to feel the pain of separation. She later remembered: "We were all surrounded by loved ones, and there stood all my little schoolmates who had come to kiss me goodbye. My father with tears in his eyes tried to smile as one friend after another grasped his hand in a last farewell. Mama was overcome with grief. At last we were in the wagon, the drivers cracked their whips, the oxen moved forward and the long journey had begun."[8]

The "jumping off place" for the journey was usually St. Joseph, Missouri, a busy, bustling town on the Missouri

River. Toward the end of April people began to gather there to buy supplies and fit up their wagons for the trip. It must have been an exciting, noisy place then—the dusty streets thronged with people, children, farm animals of all kinds.

Getting ready to go west took a lot of preparation as well as money. First, and most important, a family needed a wagon big enough to hold the family and about 2,500 pounds of food and other supplies, and sturdy enough to survive 2,000 miles of hard travel over mountains and across rivers. The wagon alone, and a team of four to six oxen to pull it, could cost $400, a very large sum of money in those days.

The *Emigrants Guide to Oregon and California,* published in 1845, advised each family to take with them "200 pounds of flour, 150 pounds of bacon, 10 pounds of coffee,

Pioneers relied on finding game along the trail to supplement the supplies they carried in their wagons.

20 pounds of sugar, and 10 pounds of salt." They also needed pots and pans, tin plates and cutlery, farm tools and rifles. In addition, most emigrants brought with them seed and farm animals with which to begin a new life.

When all was in readiness, each wagon swung out to join the huge stream of wagons, people, and animals moving westward. Rebecca Ketcham described the scene: " All around us on each side of the river were sheep, cattle, horses, wagons, men, women and children—more cattle and sheep than I ever saw in my life: drove after drove, thousands, yes, tens of thousands. . . . It is astonishing to see what a multitude is moving on."[9] In 1852, a reporter for the *New York Tribune* described the sight he called "the greatest show on earth. The train is estimated to be 700 miles long, composed of people from all parts of the United States, and

Deep ruts were carved by the wheels of many wagon trains along the Oregon Trail.

some of the rest of mankind, with lots of horses, mules, oxen, cows, steers and some of the feathered creation, moving along about 15 or 20 miles per day."[10] By 1855, the trail had been traveled by so many wagons, feet, and hooves that it was a hundred feet wide. The deep ruts made by the wagons can still be seen today.

2

NOT A TRIP FOR THE FAINTHEARTED

I write on my lap with the wind rocking the wagon," wrote Algeline Ashley in her diary, while crossing the plains in 1852. We know what this journey was like because so many of the women who went west kept diaries and journals of the trip. Some women must have known that the journey they were embarking on had historical importance. Some probably just recorded the journey for their children and grandchildren. A woman might use the time after putting her children to sleep in the wagon to crouch by the firelight and scribble her record of the day's events: how many miles traveled; how many rivers crossed; how hungry or thirsty they were; the trees and rocks, flowers and animals they saw along the way; the death of a loved one. Their detailed records bring the journey alive for us.

If the families who embarked on the journey west had known what dangers and hardships were in store for them, many might never have gone at all. Most of them were completely unprepared for the hard life of the trail. Just riding in a wagon without springs over rough and rocky

May 30th came on to Platt river again and past a traders tent of french an indians. a goodlooking white man with A black squaw for a bosom companion May past three trading post to day, and indians more than A few: stopt half way to the river and get water out of a spring, the half starved indian gethered around us, and met to day 6 large covered wagons loaded with fur wanted to swap mocasons and beads for bread and we got some, June 2nd we laid by to day to get blacksmith work done, it has been one of the windyest days ever blow'd, an A hail, and thunder storm at night, 4 indian graves were put up near us, and the hungry indians has been with us all day, I gave them a quart of gravy that was left and some scraps of bread, and they scraped into a sack. it leather one I should suppose, we threw the dogs some dirty crumbs, and they drove them away, and picked them up, and they went all around the camp and picked up the bacon rines we threw away, June 3rd come on to day about miles: and here was 7 or 8 log hu and a bakery and store, and whites and indians all together here was flour for sale for 20 dollars per sack.

This is a page from the diary of Sarah Sutton, which she kept while traveling along the Oregon Trail in 1854.

ground was uncomfortable enough. Catherine Sager remembered that "the motion made us all sick and the uncomfortableness of the situation was increased from the fact that it had set into rain, which made it impossible to roll back the cover and let in the fresh air. It also caused a damp and musty smell that was very nauseating. It took several weeks of travel to overcome this 'sea sickness.'"[1]

The work was endless and backbreaking and every family member was expected to pitch in. Women and girls did the cooking; packed, unpacked, and aired out bedding; tried to keep the wagons clean; and, whenever possible, washed pounds and pounds of clothes.

Every task that had been manageable back home was difficult on the trail. Cooking over an open fire was a particular problem. "It is very trying on the patience to cook and bake on a little green wood fire with the smoke blowing in your eyes so as to blind you, and shivering with cold so as to make the teeth chatter," wrote eighteen-year-old Esther Hanna.[2] Water and wood or buffalo dung, called

When a wagon train stopped at night, meals were usually cooked over an open fire.

chips, had to be hauled for every meal, pots and food were constantly falling into the fire, and when it rained hard, no cooking could be done at all. One man watched a woman struggling to bake bread in a rainstorm while holding an umbrella over the fire!

Laundry was an enormous task that could only be done when the train stopped long enough by a river. The combination of harsh lye soap, icy water, wind, and sun turned the skin raw. Rebecca Ketcham wrote: "Camilla and I both burnt our arms very badly while washing. . . . They were red and swollen and painful as though scalded with boiling water . . . and I do not see that there is any way of preventing it, for everything has to be done in the wind and sun."[3]

The men's work was to drive the teams; round up, feed, and water the animals; mend broken wagon wheels and axles; and hunt for game if there was any around. As soon as they were old enough, young boys were expected to "watch the stock," which meant walking at the back of the wagon to keep an eye on the herds of animals traveling with the train. Girls were expected to stay close to the wagon to help with the women's work. One woman remembered how resentful she felt when "Mother would make me get into the wagon and amuse little Frank. . . . I would feel myself very much abused, preferring to walk."[4] Even the younger children were expected to collect buffalo chips for fuel as they walked along the trail.

Weather conditions were often extreme, and the wagons offered little protection. Elizabeth Geer wrote in her diary: "It rains and it snows. . . . I carry my babe and lead, or rather carry, another through snow, mud, water, almost to my knees. It is the worst road. . . . I went ahead with my

22

children and I was afraid to look behind me for fear of seeing the wagons turn over into the mud. . . . My children gave out with cold and fatigue and could not travel, and the boys had to unhitch the oxen and bring them and carry the children on to camp. I was so cold and numb I could not tell by feeling that I had any feet at all . . . there was not one dry thread on one of us—not even my babe. . . . I have not told you half we suffered."[5]

In her lively diary written on the trail, Amelia Knight described a terrifying storm: "We had just encamped on a large flat prairie when the storm commenced in all its fury . . . the wind was so high I thought it would tear the wagons to pieces . . . and in less than two hours, the water was a foot deep all over our camping ground."[6]

Crossing a river was a particularly dangerous event for the travelers. Lodisa Frizzell, about to cross the Platte, described what she saw: "The river here is all of one mile & a half wide, & a more foaming, maddening river I never saw, & its banks being very low, & the water the color of soapsuds . . . this swift current makes an awful noise, you cannot make a person hear you, when you are in the river, at 5 yds. distant; and I call this one of the greatest adventures on the whole route."[7] Hundreds of wagons might be lined up waiting to be conducted across the treacherous currents, often by Indian guides.

Amelia Knight tells how the Elkhorn River was crossed: "There are three hundred or more wagons in sight and as far as the eye can reach the bottom is covered, on each side of the river, with cattle and horses. There is no ferry here and the men will have to make one out of the tightest wagon-beds. . . . Everything must now be hauled out of the wagon head over heels . . . then the wagon must

Sometimes wagons could be pulled across a river by means of a rope ferry.

be all taken to pieces, and then by means of a strong rope stretched across the river with a tight wagon-bed attached to the middle of it, the rope must be long enough to pull from side to side, with men on each side of the river to pull it. In this way we have to cross the river everything a little at a time. Women and children last, and then swim the cattle and horses. There were three horses and some cattle drowned while crossing this place yesterday."[8] As serious as it was to lose livestock, every family felt grateful to have gotten across a river without losing a loved one to the swift and deadly currents.

And there were other dangers. Young children were bitten by poisonous snakes, or drowned during river crossings, or fell out of their wagons and were crushed under the wheels. Many were injured or killed in buffalo stampedes, which seemed to come out of nowhere. Catherine Haun, a young bride traveling west, described one:

"One day a herd came in our direction like a great black cloud, a threatening, moving mountain, advancing toward us very swiftly and with wild snorts, noses almost to the ground and tails flying in midair . . . they . . . made a deafening, terrible noise. As is their habit when stampeding, they did not turn out of their course for anything. Some of our wagons were within the line of their advance . . . one was completely demolished and two were overturned. Several persons were hurt, one child's shoulder being dislocated, but fortunately no one was killed."[9]

When children got lost, which was easy to do on a wagon train, it could be a serious matter. Amelia Knight almost lost her daughter for good when the wagon train moved out without her. "Not a soul had missed her until we stopped a while to rest the cattle; just then another train drove up behind us with Lucy. She was terribly frightened and so were [we] when we found out what a narrow escape she had run."[10] Another little girl was visiting in her grandmother's wagon when her parents, a few wagons ahead, decided to turn off at a fork in the trail. She didn't see her parents again for two years.

By far the worst danger of the journey was sickness. In those days, people didn't have the medicines we have now, so even measles, mumps, or pneumonia could kill people. In 1849, a terrible epidemic of cholera swept across the country, killing thousands of people. Some wagon trains lost two-thirds of their people, and sometimes whole families were wiped out. One woman, Jane Kellogg, reported that "all along the road up the Platte River was a grave yard; most any time of day you could see people burying their dead; some places five or six graves in a row, with board head signs with their names carved on them. It was a sad sight; no one can realize it unless they had seen it."[11]

The emigrants feared Indians most of all, even though in fact more people were killed by disease and accidents than by Indians. As Virginia Donner wrote after her safe arrival in California, "We suffered vastly more from fear of the Indians *before* starting than we did on the plains."[12] In the early years especially, most Indians were simply curious about these strange new people in their country, and eager to trade with them. Sometimes misunderstandings arose because the emigrants didn't understand Indian customs. For example, one woman complained that though "these prairie redmen were generally friendly, they were insistent beggars, often following us for miles and at mealtimes disgustingly stood around and solicited food."[13] She didn't know that among Indian tribes sharing food was a sign of friendship and hospitality.

Indians did attack wagon trains, however, and Catherine Haun described how they protected themselves: "When going into camp, the 'leader wagon' was turned from the road to the right, the next wagon to the left, the others following close after and always alternating to right and left. In this way, a large circle, or corral was formed within which the tents were pitched and the oxen herded. The horses were picketed nearby until bed-time, when they were tethered to the tongues of the wagons."[14]

Helen Carpenter, who crossed the plains in 1857,

recorded this harrowing incident in her diary: "When the sun was just peeping over the top of the mountains, there was suddenly heard a shot and a blood curdling yell, and immediately the Indians we saw yesterday were seen riding directly toward the horses. . . . Father put his gun to his shoulder as though to shoot. . . . The Indians kept . . . circling . . . and halooing . . . bullets came whizzing through the camp. None can know the horror of it."[15] Evidently the Indians meant only to terrify the travelers, because when Helen's father and brother began shooting, the Indians moved off.

3

SEEING THE ELEPHANT

When they got to the South Pass, deep in the Rocky Mountains, the emigrants were halfway to their destination. The South Pass was the easiest route through the mountains. Here, the wagon trains divided. One group took the northerly route along the Snake River, through the Blue Mountains, to Oregon. The other group traveled along the Humboldt River, across the dreadful Humboldt Sink, and through the Sierra Nevada to California. Now both groups were feeling the pressure of time. It was urgent to get through the mountains before the first snows came, which could happen as early as September. To be caught in the mountains in a snowstorm could be fatal.

Crossing the mountains was a terrifying experience. To begin with, almost all the pioneers' wagons were too heavy, loaded down with everything they thought they might need in their new life. As soon as they started up their first mountain, they found they had to unload precious possessions and leave them by the wayside. Travelers told of seeing all kinds of discarded objects along the narrow mountain paths: rocking chairs, cookstoves, crates of china and books, even children's toys.

Even after they were lightened, the wagons often had to be hauled up a mountain with ropes and chains. But if going up was hard work, coming down was even worse. Catherine Haun, making the journey in 1849, described in her diary getting across the Rocky Mountains: "Sometimes to keep the wagons from pressing upon the animals in going down grade, young pine trees were cut down and . . . tied to the front and under the rear axle. The branches dragging upon the ground, or often on solid rock, formed a reliable brake. Then again, a rope or chain would be tied to the rear of the wagon and everyone, man, woman and child would be pressed into service to hold the wagon back."[1]

Sometimes a wagon would break its chains and go tumbling down the steep slope, splintering into pieces as it went, and taking with it all a family's possessions.

The emigrants had an expression, "seeing the elephant," which meant having a disastrous, unexpected ending to a once-in-a-lifetime adventure. The expression came from a joke about the old one-horse peddler who went to the city on the day the circus arrived because he had never seen an elephant. When the elephants walked by, his horse leaped in the air, turning the wagon upside down and spilling all the wares in the road. A man who stopped to help said, "That's too bad. I'm afraid your business is ruined." The old peddler exclaimed, "It's all right. I have finally seen an elephant!"

For those who took the overland route to California, that "seeing the elephant" moment usually came in the

Humboldt Sink, a scorching, fifty-mile desert covered with fine, harsh alkali dust that got into your eyes, nose, and mouth. It was here that most of the domestic animals the travelers had brought with them perished. Catherine Haun described this as the worst part of the entire trip. "It was no unusual sight to see graves, carcasses of animals and abandoned wagons. . . . Animals often perished or were so overcome by heat and exhaustion that they had to be abandoned, or in cases of human hunger, the poor jaded creatures were killed and eaten."[2]

In spite of the danger and hardships, there was excite-

Wagon trains crossing the arid Humboldt Sink in Nevada often lost a large number of their animals, which died of heat and thirst.

ment, pleasure, and even fun on the journey. Catherine Haun and her party reached "the beautiful Laramie River" on the Fourth of July. "Its sparkling, pure waters were full of myriads of fish that could be caught with scarcely an effort. . . . After dinner that night it was proposed that we celebrate the day and we all heartily joined in. . . . We sang patriotic songs, repeated what little we could of the Declaration of Independence, fired off a gun or two, and gave three cheers for the United States and California Territory in particular!"[3]

Many travelers were awed by the natural wonders they saw along the way. Independence Rock, a huge, turtle-shaped rock formation near the Sweetwater River, was one such marvel. So many passing travelers inscribed their names on it that one pioneer called it "the bulletin board of the Sweetwater Valley."[4]

Emigrants carved their names into rocks along the trail, as shown in this photo of Register Cliff, Wyoming.

For young people, the journey could be the adventure of a lifetime. Susan Parrish, who was seventeen when she made the journey in 1850, remembered: "We were a happy, carefree lot of young people, and the dangers and hardships found no resting place on our shoulders. It was a continuous picnic and excitement was plentiful. . . . In the evenings, we gathered around the campfires and played games or told stories."[5] Caroline Richardson and her friends had a snowball fight at South Pass in the Rocky Mountains, and when they reached Salt Lake City they "pitched a tent in a potato patch . . . found a fiddler . . . and danced till eleven."[6]

But after so many months of travel, most of the emigrants could think only of getting to their destination. "I am so anxious to get some place to stop and settle that my patience isn't worth much," wrote one woman in her diary.[7] And Jane Gould Tortillot, longing to join her relatives in California, burst out, "Oh dear, I do so want to get there. It is now four months since we have slept in a house. If I could only be set down at home with all the folks I think there would be some talking as well as resting."[8]

Catherine Thomas Morrison crossed the country with her parents and seven brothers and sisters in 1849. Her memory of how they felt when they arrived in the Willamette Valley captures the relief and delight that many of the travelers must have felt.

"I can't hope to explain to you how happy we all were. Father and Mother and all eight of us children had crossed the plains in good health. We children were particularly happy, for, instead of having to strike out each morning and walk barefooted in the dust, where we stubbed our toes, stepped on cactus and watched that we didn't step on any rattlesnakes, we were in a country where the grass was belly-deep for the cattle and when the sea-breeze made it wave it looked like waves of changeable green silk. We didn't have to worry about the Indians running off our stock. No longer did we have to eat bacon, beans, and camp bread, and not get as much of any of them as we wanted, for here we had found a country of beauty, where we could have all the vegetables we wanted, where the hills were full of deer, and the streams full of trout, where, when we looked to the westward, instead of seeing nothing but a long, winding train of prairie schooners with a cloud of dust hanging over all, we saw waving grass and vividly green fir trees . . . and to the eastward we could see Mount Hood, clean and clear and beautiful and so wonderful that it almost took your breath."[9]

4

SETTLING IN

As happy as the travelers were to arrive safely at their destination, they soon found out that starting a new life was not so easy. Farming, of course, could not begin until a family had a home, and most emigrants arrived at the beginning of winter, too late to build their own homes. They had to move in with other families in already crowded quarters. That first winter was long and hard. Marilla Washburn, who was eleven years old when she came to Oregon, had lost her brother on the journey: "My most vivid recollection of that first winter in Oregon is of the weeping skies and of Mother and me also weeping."[1]

Other families were shocked by their first glimpse of their new home. When Mary Jones, whose husband had gone ahead to find a homestead, arrived at the place he'd chosen, she saw "nothing in sight but nature . . . nothing . . . except a little mud and stick hut."[2] Another woman remembered the look on her mother's face when they arrived at the log cabin her husband had built: "Without a word, she crossed its threshold, and, standing very still, looked slowly around her. . . . She could not realize even then, I think, that this was really the place father had prepared for us, that here he expected us to live . . . her face never lost the deep lines those first hours of pioneer life had cut upon it."[3]

But many women would have been grateful to find a log cabin ready for them at the end of the journey. Sara McAllister's mother made her husband hollow out two giant tree stumps in Washington's Nisqually Valley and moved into them with her six children while her husband built their house. "She found it very comfortable," Sara remembered, "the burnt-out roots making such nice cubby-

A giant hollow tree could provide a temporary home.

holes for storing away things."[4] Other families lived in caves, dugouts, tents, and houses made entirely of wagon canvas.

The new settlers could usually count on help from their neighbors in building their first house. The men worked in teams cutting logs out of trees to make a framework. Then the frame was raised into place by ropes attached to the beams, with everyone pulling on them. The three days it took to raise a log cabin was also a time for families to get together for fun, conversation, and games. Once the cabin was built, the whole family, including the children, "chinked," or filled the cracks between the logs with mud, grass, straw, or whatever material was available.

Since there were no sawmills to make smooth boards, floors were often made of dirt or gravel. "Have you done your house-raking today?" one housewife might ask another.[5] Furnishings had to be improvised, using whatever was handy. One Oregon woman described how she and her husband managed: "My husband made a table of split boards, and I went to work making stools, which I cushioned with moss and covered with oiled calico. I made a rocking chair out of a sugar barrel, cushioned and covered it the same way. Cupboards and other conveniences I also manufactured. I was very proud of my new home."[6]

Unless a family had brought along their mattresses, bedding also had to be improvised. Some people used prairie grass, buffalo hair, or corn husks for bedding. A Mormon settler named Priscilla Merriman Evans remembered: "We went down to the marshy land and gathered a load of cattails, which I stripped and made me a good bed and pillows. They were as soft as feathers."[7]

Settlers from several families would work together to build a log cabin.

Glass for windows was a great luxury because it was so hard to get. This was a problem because the Homestead Act required that a house have at least one glass window in order for the family to "prove up" its claim. Elizabeth Gedney, an Oregon woman, described how several families would go in together to buy one glass window for them all to share: "As a man got ready to prove up on his claim he borrowed the window, put it up and invited the inspectors. After their visit, he took the window down, put it under the bed ready for the next homesteader, and nailed up a sheep hide to keep the wind out."[8]

When the newcomers looked around for promising sites for their farms, they often came into conflict with the Indians who were already living there. In Henry Shepard's case, the problem was resolved without violence. His daughter, Elizabeth, who was twelve at the time, later remembered: "In the Spring of 1853 Father took up for his . . . claim a beautiful, grassy, level meadow about two miles west of The Dalles, near Mill Creek. Just above our place was an Indian camp. Father put in a garden. The Indian chief who was camped above us told us that Father had settled on their grazing land, and that they had lived there and used it so long that the oldest Indian couldn't remember when they weren't there. Of course, Father didn't want to give up the place, so Mark, the Indian chief, went to Major Alvord at the Dalles and asked him to make us get off their land. Major Alvord sent some soldiers to help us move our things off the Indian's land. The soldiers and the Indians moved our household goods down to the river bank."[9]

This was a rare instance in which the U.S. Army actually sided with the Indians. As time went on, and more and more settlers moved onto Indian lands, the army almost always sided with the homesteaders against the Indians.

Sara McAllister and her family came to Washington in 1845 with five other families, including that of George William Bush, the first black settler in what became

Washington Territory. The party had intended to settle in Oregon, but when they got word that any black who entered Oregon would be whipped, they agreed to continue north of the Columbia River. Sara's father, James, struck up a friendship with the chief of the Nisqually Indians, Leschi, who invited him to settle in the Nisqually Valley. By 1855, many new settlers had poured into the valley, and relations between them and the Nisquallies had become hostile. Chief Leschi, accompanied by his two wives, paid a visit to the McAllister family.

"He told us that he was going to fight," remembered Sara. "Father and mother both tried to persuade him to remain peaceful. . . . The women talked and cried together.

Chief Leschi

He told father that if he would remain on the farm and not join the army, he should not be hurt or his property destroyed."[10] However, Sara's father did join the army and was killed by Nisqually Indians in an ambush.

Soon afterward, Nisquallies surrounded the McAllister home. Sara, her mother, and her brothers and sister managed to escape in a wagon. "The wagon had to cross the reservation in order to reach the fort. With one boy driving the oxen, and one behind, we started beating the oxen into a run. The road was fearful. . . . And we were looking for the Indians to be on us at any moment."[11] By the time they reached the safety of the fort, the children were in a state of terror. "So tight had been our grasp upon the chain across the wagon box, that the soldiers had to unclasp our hands from it, as we were unable to do so ourselves; our little bodies were so bruised and bleeding, that we were unable to stand on our feet."[12]

In a way, the history of the McAllister family resembles the changing relationship between the American Indians and the pioneers in general. At first, many tribes welcomed the newcomers, trading with them and showing them how to live in the new land. But as time went on, and the homesteaders took over more and more of their land, Indians stopped trusting the settlers and began to see them as enemies. This led to terrible fighting and massacres in which both Indians and settlers were killed. Although it took many years of bloody battles and persuasion, in the end the settlers succeeded in driving the Indians off most of the lands they had lived on for centuries.

STARTING FROM SCRATCH

Most of the homesteaders who went west to farm and ranch had no idea of the difficulties they would encounter. Farming had always been hard work, but back east it had been a straightforward matter of ploughing the fields, planting seed, and harvesting crops. The new land presented a variety of challenges, problems, and unexpected disasters.

The first thing the homesteaders found out about farming in the new land was that there was so much work to be done that the dividing line between "women's work" and "men's work" often broke down. Men hauled water for their wives on wash day and sometimes helped plant and irrigate the family garden. More often, a wife would be called upon to help her husband in the field. "Tarpley made a furrow with a single-shovel plow drawn by one horse," explained Elmira Taylor, remembering farming in the 1860s. "I followed with a bag of seed corn and dropped two grains of seed each step forward."[1]

Sometimes husband and wife were both learning to do things they'd never had to do before. Priscilla Merriman Evans, the wife of a Mormon minister, who migrated to Utah in 1856, wrote: "My husband had never driven a team before he came to Utah. He . . . knew nothing about any kind of work but his profession as [preacher]. His hands were soft and white, but he soon wore blisters . . . in learning to make adobes, digging ditches, making roads, driving oxen, and doing what was required of pioneers in a new country."[2]

Women who came from towns and cities back east found they had to make literally everything from scratch as there were no places to buy the things they needed. Long before any cooking was done, a farm wife had to raise chickens, milk cows, plant and tend a large garden, can, dry, and preserve the vegetables and fruit that grew in the garden, make butter and cheese, grind corn or wheat into flour for bread, and help slaughter livestock and prepare the meat.

Cooking began well before sunup, and often consisted of five meals a day. First, there was a huge breakfast for the men going out to the fields. A snack of some kind had to be prepared to be taken out to the men at midmorning. Another large meal was served at 1:30, another midafternoon snack, and supper at sundown. At harvesttime, when as many as twenty-five men might be working at one farm, farm wives pooled their pots and pans, dishes, and labor. Newly washed dishes never even saw the inside of the cupboard—they were simply set back on the table for the next meal. Since bread and pies had to be baked four and five times a day, ovens were hot all day long, so many women baked in sheds or shacks apart from the house.

An oven might be in use all day long, so it was frequently located in a shed outside the home.

Pioneer children started working almost as soon as they could walk. At first they worked close to home, under their mother's supervision, doing such jobs as collecting eggs, watering and feeding the animals, hauling water, and weeding the garden.

As children grew older, the boys tended to start working in the fields with their fathers, while the girls remained with their mothers, learning women's tasks such as cooking, sewing, laundry, and soap making. However, girls growing up in pioneer families had more freedom to do other kinds of work than they might have had growing up back east. Fathers who needed hands in the fields often called upon their daughters to help. And of course, fathers who had only daughters had no choice but to put them to work in the fields. Elenore Plaisted's tenth birthday fell during harvesttime and she spent it "driving a span of

Pioneer children were expected to help with the farm work.

huge farm horses to and fro between the thrashers and the granary and feeling very important."[3]

In the beginning, homesteaders helped one another by trading and sharing work, tools, and produce. Priscilla Merriman Evans described how this worked among the early Mormon settlers: "My husband . . . worked for William Markham a year, for which he received two acres of land. I helped in the house, for which, beside the land, we got our board and keep. The next Spring we went to work for ourselves. We saved two acres of wheat, and made adobes for a two-roomed house, and paid a man in adobes for laying it up. . . . If one neighbor had something they could get along without, they would exchange it for something they could use. . . . We raised a good crop of wheat that fall, for which we traded one bushel of potatoes. We also exchanged for molasses and vegetables. . . . I traded for a hen . . . and I have never been without chickens in all of my married life since."[4]

Marianne Hunsaker D'Arcy, whose family emigrated to Oregon in the 1840s, remembered that her mother made soap that she traded for a hen. "Together with Eliza Gordon . . . she bought a rooster. They raised chickens, taking the little chickens from the hens as soon as they were hatched so the hen would go to laying sooner. We never ate an egg. They were all to be saved. Mother raised 102 chickens the first year from her hen and the daughters of the hen. Mrs. Gordon raised nearly 100. This gave them the money to buy cloth to make dresses for themselves and their girls."[5]

Often people found they couldn't grow the kind of crops they had expected to. Farmers in the Pacific Northwest, for example, discovered that the climate was inhospitable to corn. They were also unprepared for the chinook—a hot, dry wind that came howling down from the Rocky Mountains in the spring. Within a day, a chinook could turn a ripening field into acres of dry, withered stalks.

Most horrifying of all were the clouds of grasshoppers and crickets that seemed to appear out of nowhere and swarmed over farms, destroying everything in their path— even the laundry hanging on a line. "Wingless, dumpy, black, swollen-headed, with bulging eyes in cases like goggles, mounted upon legs of steel wire and clock spring . . . a cross of the spider on the buffalo," is how a Mormon historian of the time described the crickets that overran the shores of the Great Salt Lake.[6]

Homesteader Elizabeth Roe described a grasshopper invasion: "They came down like great clouds and settled all over the farm and a garden and on the peach trees which were not far from the house. They ate all the leaves off and devoured the bark of the small limbs, there being hundreds on quite a small twig. They destroyed all our sweet corn in a few hours the first day and still they came—the earth was literally covered with them. I saw heaps of grasshoppers as large as a washtub. They commenced on a forty-acre field about ten o'clock and before night there was not an ear of corn or green leaf to be seen."[7]

For homesteaders on the Great Plains, water was the biggest problem. There just wasn't much around in the form of lakes, ponds, or streams, and the annual rainfall was very low compared to the East. As a result, a farmer had to till much more land in order to get the same amount of crops he had gotten back home. Every drop of rain was precious, so after each rainfall, farmers learned to "har-

Farmers faced swarms of grasshoppers that could wipe out an entire field of corn in a day.

row" their fields, turning over the soil so that the moisture was stored near the plants' roots, instead of evaporating in the sun. Until the late 1860s, when the "chilled-iron plow" and the spring-toothed harrow were invented, the soil had to be broken by hand, which was backbreaking work.

Even water for household use often had to be hauled from great distances. J. C. Ruppenthal, a pioneer on the plains of western Kansas, remembered that "the spring, about a half a mile or more distant, was the nearest source of good water. . . . A yoke was made to place across the shoulders, so as to carry at each end a bucket, and then water was brought a half a mile from spring to house. Both father and mother carried water thus from day to day."[8]

LONGHORNS AND WOOLLIES

Lack of water was not such a big problem, however, for other kinds of homesteaders who began to settle in the plains and desert regions beyond the Rocky Mountains. These dry, grassy lands, so hard to farm, were just right for ranchers with their huge herds of animals.

Ranching didn't get started in earnest until after the Civil War. Until then, the plains were dominated by Indian tribes and the herds of buffalo they lived on. By the 1860s, most of the buffalo had been killed, and the Indians were gradually being driven off the plains. This opened up vast new areas of the country for settlement.

The Homestead Act of 1862 allowed a head of family or a male over twenty-one to claim 160 acres of public land as long as he or she lived on and cultivated the land for five years. In 1877, the Desert Land Act was passed, which offered 640 acres of land at $1.25 an acre to anyone who would irrigate some portion of it. Some cattlemen got around the law by rounding up witnesses who would swear they'd seen water on the land—usually a pail of water thrown on the ground.

Although there was some cattle ranching in Washington and Oregon Territories, the earliest ranchers settled farther south, in what is now Southern California, Nevada, New Mexico, and Texas. Later, Montana, Idaho, and Wyoming also drew ranchers.

Adolf Fuchs, a German teacher who immigrated to America in 1845 with his family, was an early settler in Texas, where he planned to take up ranching. He wrote to his neighbors back home: "Getting the water on our place is inconvenient as it is located about 500 to 600 paces from the house; however, we already have a sled with a barrel and we are negotiating for a horse. Later we can dig a well."[1] Adolf traded his family's fine table linen and some German rifles for cattle and was very pleased with his bargain. "Livestock does not require any work," he wrote. "It is a joy to watch our cows and calves coming to the pen every evening. So far Lulu [his wife] milks the cows, but shortly she will have Ulla as a helper and then Ottilie."[2] Ulla and Ottilie were his daughters.

Although Adolf Fuchs was a hard worker, he had never farmed before and he was unused to handling a plow at first. His daughter Ottilie sympathized. "How clumsy and difficult it all was for the hands better suited to the use of a violin bow or at most a pair of garden shears," she wrote.[3] Fortunately, his American neighbors took pity on him and plowed his land in return for his promise to teach their children.

Emma Marble, as a bride-to-be, took advantage of the Desert Land Act to homestead in New Mexico. Under the law, a married woman could not stake her own claim, but a

Plowing a prairie

single woman could. "John and I were not yet married, so I filed a claim and in the center of the hundred and sixty acres that I chose were the shanty, the corral, the cottonwood tree and the well."[4]

Like all settlers in the Southwest, Emma's primary concern was water and how to move it from well and pond to house and garden. The Marbles used a windmill. "John had enlarged the shanty to two rooms, and had run a water pipe from the well to the kitchen door. . . . We also had a garden. . . . The soil produced bountifully under irrigation from the earth tank into which the windmill pumped the water. "[5]

Agnes Morley Cleaveland remembered her childhood on a Texas cattle ranch in the early 1900s. "As youngsters we learned to recognize the individuals among the cattle as though they had been people. . . . We knew our own dry cows or long yearlings or three-year-old heifers as city children know their schoolmates."[6]

Once the first transcontinental railroad was completed in 1869, cattle could be shipped back east for sale. Cattle were cheap: a Texas longhorn could be purchased for only $7 or $8. Once a rancher had assembled a herd, he or she hired cowboys who drove the herd, usually about 3,000 head of cattle, hundreds of dusty miles north to Abilene, Wichita, or some other Kansas cattle town. There the cows were sold, often for $50 or $60 each.

It could take two or three months to drive a herd from Texas to Kansas. At the end of the trail, weary, grimy cowboys would make a beeline for town and a hot bath, shave, and haircut. Clean and spruced up, and with money in their pockets, the cowboys often headed first to a photography studio before setting out for a night on the town.

Cora Clark, whose family settled in the Willamette Valley of Oregon, remembered that in the 1870s "the cattle trail went past our farm and the cowboys always bedded down on some vacant land near us so they could be near water. They would come to the house and get milk and other provisions. One of the most wonderful sights of my childhood was 10,000 head of cattle being driven to Cheyenne."[7]

By 1880, huge herds of longhorn cattle were crossing the plains of the West, from Montana to New Mexico. With so much land and so many cattle drifting across property lines to graze, ranchers had to find ways of figuring out whose cattle was whose. Each owner branded his newborn calves with his own mark. Every spring and fall, thousands of cattle were rounded up and driven into one area.

Cowboys had to handle a large number of cattle on a cattle drive.

Cowboys working for each ranch rode through the huge herds, separating out each rancher's cattle. "The busiest time on a ranch is the preparation for the spring roundups," remembered a Texas cowboy. "There are saddles to mend, hobbles to make, grub wagons to overhaul and horses to get in shape, shoeing and trimming up, quirts [short, braided leather whips] to make, ropes to straighten up and planning till you can't rest."[8] When barbed wire was invented in 1873, it became easier for ranchers to fence their property and protect their stock.

Most people tend to think of cowboys as white, mostly because they're usually played by white actors in Hollywood Westerns. In reality, at least a quarter of all American cowboys were black, and close to another quarter were Mexican. A typical eight-man crew on a long cattle drive might include three or four black or Mexican cowboys. The foreman, however, was almost always white. One black cowboy, who was famous for his riding and roping skills, remarked, "If it weren't for my damned old black face, I'd have been a boss long ago."[9] The white cowboys he worked with agreed.

Prejudice against Mexican cowboys flared up as well. "The way to handle a Mexican," said one Texan, "is to kick 'em in the ribs."[10] But generally cowboys in a crew treated one another with respect as long as each man did his job.

There were even a few cow*girls*, or maybe cow*women* would be a better term. In the late 1800s in Idaho, a young woman named Jo Monaghan disguised herself as a man and became a skilled and respected wrangler. At around the same time, a woman named Lizzie Johnson and her husband, Hezekiah, drove separate herds up the cattle trail. Lizzie became one of the first women to register her own brand.

During the 1870s, sheep ranchers began to move into California, New Mexico, Wyoming, and Montana. Back east, people had heard that sheep were cheap to buy and easy to raise. The prospect of an adventurous life in the open lured young people like Otto Merdian, a twenty-two-year-old clerk in a dry goods store in Alton, Illinois. In 1882 he and his cousin, Ed Adam, and his dog, Don, struck out for Montana. In his lively letters to his sister back home, Otto told of the beautiful scenery he had passed on the journey and shooting his first antelope. He even enclosed samples of unfamiliar wildflowers he had picked along the way.

After several false starts, Otto, Ed, and Don settled on Sweet Grass Creek. He wrote to his sister, "I think we have got a good piece of land for sheep. There are a row of hills north that will break the north winds and will be a good place to let the sheep run on in the winter. The wind blows all the snow off of the hills so the sheep can eat the dry grass."[11]

Otto laid out his plan to go to California or Oregon to buy sheep. "We can buy them for $1.50 & $1.75 a head there and drive them over. The only expense is I will have to get a pony to go on. [I] can drive them over in a year and a half, and while I am gone, Ed will do the farm work so we can make things work in that way. Ed will have to get sheds built for them, hay put up, and everything ready for them. [In California] we can get twice as many and there will be no more expense. The wool pays all the expenses, and they can graze on the way just as well as if they were in this part of the country."[12]

By the 1880s, cattle ranchers found they had to share their ranges with sheep, and they didn't like it. The ranges were already overcrowded with cattle, and the cattlemen thought the sheep ruined the grass by close-cropping it. Soon cowboys and sheepherders started fighting each other. Many men were killed or hurt, and hundreds of thousands of sheep were shot or driven over cliffs.

But even some cattle ranchers switched from cattle to "woollies," as they were sometimes called. Adolf Fuchs's daughter Ottilie and her husband, Carl Goeth, decided to raise sheep. She later wrote: "Sheep-raising was . . . more complicated than the inexperienced might think. It requires experience and patience to care for the large herds, to protect them against disease, to provide them with good grazing land and water, also to protect them from the wolves and then to count them each evening in order to determine if any were lost. During the lambing season Carl was particularly busy keeping the mother sheep and young lambs together. Every sheep and lamb had a number painted on its side so that the sheepherders could assist the mother sheep in keeping track of their little ones. . . .

"Of course, it was the greatest fun for the children when the young lambs were driven out in the mornings, and came home in the evenings, and it truly did look very gay when hundreds of lambs were hopping about. Almost every morning one could see little two-year-old Eddie in the midst of the flock, his little head barely showing above the sheep, while Uncle Otto always kept an eye on him so that he would not come to any harm.

"A particularly busy time was when the sheep were sheared in March or April. The shears clipped away many a day, while the housewife did not complain as she prepared good food in the kitchen for the men. I suppose some swollen hands had to be taken care of as well. . . . Then . . . the wagons piled high were driven to Marble Falls for sale."[13]

Ranching—especially sheep ranching—could be a lonely business for both men and women. Shepherds usually worked alone and spent long days out on the range with no company but their dog and their sheep. Their wives were often stranded in isolated cabins far from neighbors for weeks at a time. Mrs. Arthur Cowan and her husband raised sheep in Woody Island, Montana—"forty

Hand clippers were used to shear the sheep in spring.

miles from civilization, where nobody lives and dogs bark at strangers." Her diary reveals her loneliness:

"Cold windy day 24 below zero. Fed the sheep. Very lonely."

"Ten degrees below zero this morning. Have been very down-hearted today and had a very bad headache."

"Men are working at lambing. Oh I feel so lonely so sad and discontented."[14]

Emma Marble remembered, "The loneliness—it was terrible! As John and his cowhands had to be on the range all day long I was alone most of the time. I looked forward to round-up times twice a year, because John took me along in the wagon. . . . I longed for the windmill to have a breakdown so John would have to take the part—and me—to the village."[15]

Not every woman rancher was as lonely and miserable as Mrs. Cowan, however. Elinore Pruitt, a plucky young widow with a little daughter to support, was working as a laundress and housecleaner in Denver in 1909. She hired herself out as a housekeeper to a Scotch cattle rancher in Wyoming, where she planned to file a homestead claim of her own. Elinore was a woman of amazing energy and enthusiasm. In addition to managing the cattleman's household, she milked cows, made and sold butter, raised chickens, planted and tended a huge garden, and put up hundreds of jars of preserves. She even found time to take her daughter, Jerrine, on a camping trip in the mountains! Elinore also surprised her employer, Mr. Stewart, by helping him out when he was short of men at mowing time.

"I was afraid to tell him I could mow for fear he would forbid me to do so. But one morning, when he was out chasing a last hope of help, I went down to the barn, took out the horses, and went to mowing. I had enough cut before he got back to show him I knew how, and as he came back manless, he was delighted as well as surprised. I was glad because I really like to mow, and besides that, I am adding feathers to my cap in a surprising way."[16]

Clyde Stewart must have realized what a valuable partner Elinore was because they were married within a year. However, the fiercely independent Elinore insisted on filing her own claim. "I should not have married if Clyde had not promised I should meet all my land difficulties unaided. I wanted the fun and the experience."[17]

Elinore was very enthusiastic about women homesteading, but she knew it might not suit every woman. She wrote her former employer in Denver, "Persons afraid of coyotes and work and loneliness had better let ranching alone. At the same time, any woman who can stand her own company, can see the beauty of the sunset, loves growing things, and is willing to put in as much time at careful labor as she does over the washtub, will certainly succeed; will have independence, plenty to eat all the time, and a home of her own in the end."[18]

GETTING ALONG

For the first year or two, most homesteaders were too busy to think about anything besides surviving. But once their farms and ranches began to succeed, the pioneers could turn their attention to things that would make their lives a little easier and pleasanter.

One of the homesteader's biggest problems was the lack of refrigeration. This meant coming up with ways to preserve food for long periods of time. Margaret Sackett, a Wyoming rancher, remembered: "As we had no jars in which to preserve wild fruit for the winter, we cooked it to the consistency of thin paste, put it through a sieve, and dried the mixture on large platters before the open fire until it was like leather. These flat cakes were then hung from the roof beams to be taken down when needed, boiled with water and sweetened sometimes with brown sugar."[1]

Meat was usually readily available because there was so much wild game to be hunted and, on ranches, of course, plenty of beef or lamb. Meat was preserved by drying it into something called "jerky." Mrs. Wilson Barnett, who was born in Klickitat County, Oregon, in 1860, remembered another solution to the refrigeration problem: "My father would kill a beef and would divide it among the neighbors. Later, one of the neighbors would kill a beef and send it around to all his neighbors. By taking turns in this way they were able to eat a beef without having it spoil."[2]

Vegetables, especially potatoes, were important because without them people could get diseases like scurvy. Eula Precious Fisher described how her family preserved their vegetables: "We kept our vegetables in a big pot in the root cellar. We'd put straw in it and then we'd put our carrots and potatoes and squash and turnips and rutabagas. Then we'd cover them over with straw and put canvas over that and put dirt on top to hold it down. But you had to leave a little space for ventilation so they wouldn't rot. . . . Many types of vegetables—things like beans—we dried. We had to put them on canvas out somewhere off the ground so that the air could get underneath them."[3]

Wise homesteaders learned from the Indians how to find and prepare native plants. Narcissa Whitman, a missionary in the Northwest, was introduced to the camas root by the Indians. "When cooked, it is very sweet and tastes like a fig."[4] A California woman visiting a tribe of Digger Indians found the bread they made of acorns delicious until she learned they used crushed earthworms for shortening![5]

Clothing posed problems as well since, of course, there were no stores in which to buy cloth. In the beginning, homesteaders improvised by cutting up their canvas wagon covers and tents to make coats and jackets. One pioneer, Jesse Applegate, recalled that his aunt spun yarn and then made clothing out of wolves' fleece.[6] Priscilla Merriman Evans noted that "when our dresses wore thin in front, they could be turned back to front and upside down and have a new lease on life."[7]

A few women managed to bring their spinning wheels with them across the country, but most had had to abandon theirs on the journey. Oregon pioneer Catherine Thomas Morris remembered: "For my 13th birthday I was given a spinning wheel. This was in 1854. Mother was a good hand at carding wool . . . and we washed, carded, spun and wove it on shares, so we soon had plenty of clothes. Mother used alder bark to dye the cloth brown and oak bark to dye it butternut color."[8] Since making a single dress took so much work, we can imagine how Marianne Hunsaker's mother felt when, after finishing and washing a dress, she hung it on a bush to dry and "the cow discovered it and ate part of it. You don't know what a tragedy that was. . . ."[9]

Sewing—especially quilting—often provided a solution to the loneliness of a life in which the nearest neighbor might be twenty miles away. "I would have lost my mind if I had not had my quilts to do,"[10] wrote one farm woman. Women would travel for miles to one woman's house to piece quilts together. Women who had been alone for months at a time treasured these "quilting bees" as times when they could enjoy laughing, gossiping, and sharing information and support with other women.

Homesickness was another problem. Homesteaders yearned for news of the families they'd left behind, but mail could take as long as three years to travel by boat down around Cape Horn. Mary Richardson Walker, a missionary in Oregon, did not learn of her mother's death until nearly two years after it happened. People filled their letters with all kinds of things—photographs, seeds, dried

Pioneer women could use a spinning wheel to spin wool and weave it into material for clothes.

flowers, locks of hair, bits of dresses, and gold pieces. "I will enclose a small piece of my wedding cake," wrote Rachel Biles to her sisters the day after she was married.[11]

People found many small ways to relieve their homesickness. When Elenore Plaisted's mother, homesteading on the treeless Dakota plains, was sent a box of paints by

63

Quilting could be done alone, but often it was done during a quilting bee, when lonely pioneer women would get together for a day of sewing, eating, and talking.

her sister, she immediately painted a spray of apple blossoms, a reminder of her old home in Maine. Another woman found a single dandelion growing near her door—the seed had somehow traveled across the country with her. "I felt less lonely all that day," she remembered, and carefully cultivated the weed year after year because it reminded her of home.[12]

Women also confided their private feelings about their daily lives, their husbands, their children, their loneliness, and their accomplishments into their diaries and journals. It seemed to make them feel better just to record the small events of the day. Lucy Flake, a Mormon woman living on a windswept Arizona farm, wrote, "I will just write my morning chores. Get up, turn out my chickens, draw a pail of water, take it to Brother Whipple's chickens, let them out, then draw water, water hot beds, make a fire, put potatoes to cook, then brush and sweep half inch of dust off floor . . . feed three litters of chickens, then mix biscuits, get breakfast, milk, besides work in the house, and this morning had to go half a mile for calves. This is the way of life on the farm."[13]

Homesteaders were so desperate for human contact that they traveled enormous distances for a chance to get together with their neighbors. Weddings and holiday celebrations were usually two-day affairs, since most people had traveled so long to get to them. Tina Zumwalt Howard of Ashland, Oregon, sometimes rode forty miles on horseback with her father to dances where he played the fiddle. "In those days, the dances started right after supper. A good substantial meal was served just before midnight, and refreshments were served again at about four A.M. Refreshments in those days didn't mean a cup of tea and a sandwich. It meant all the deer meat and potatoes you could eat, as well as cakes and pie, and coffee made out of burnt rye or burnt bread crust."[14] Children were often put to bed in cots in a back room with the coats and wraps while their parents enjoyed the dance, and in the confusion of leaving, babies sometimes ended up with the wrong families!

One of Eula Precious Fisher's favorite times was her family's annual Fourth of July celebration at a place they called the "Two-Cannon River." She wrote, "Everyone who lived for miles around would come, all the families, would come in wagons and they'd pitch their tents out there on the grounds, and they'd bring food and clothing to last them from the 3d to the 5th of July. . . . It'd take us maybe a day and a half to drive our team up there—we'd camp overnight on the way. . . . Everynight there'd be dancing with old time fiddlers and when the children got tired, they'd take 'em to their tents and put 'em to bed and then come back and dance some more. During the day we'd have horse races and foot races and the men would throw horse shoes—I remember that sound of horse shoes ringing out all over the campground. The women would mostly just sit around and visit mainly. Well, that was really the highlight of the year for us."[15]

Christmas, of course, was the most important holiday of all for many homesteaders. Pioneer families far from their old homes and loved ones had to invent new ways of celebrating this beloved holiday. If there were no fir trees to be found, they substituted a cottonwood or hung boughs of scrub sage from the ceiling. They decorated with whatever was around or could be made by hand: strings of popcorn or berries, corn husks, chains of paper loops, bits of cloth and ribbon, and candles. One woman remembered fondly "the most delightful odor of scorching cedar" as her father walked around the tree "smothering every smoking stem and keeping the candles burning safely."[16]

Even on isolated Texas ranches, a big dance was usually held at Christmas or New Year's. Since there were never enough women to go around, cowboys danced with each other, one cowboy tying a handkerchief or "heifer brand" around his sleeve to signify he was the "lady" partner.

William Bollaert described a Christmas candy-pull he attended on the Texas frontier in 1843: "A quantity of molasses is boiled down until it becomes thick; it is then

A dance was a big event on isolated ranches, even though there might not be any women partners there.

poured out onto dishes and plates, each one taking a portion in their hands and commence 'pulling,' or elongating it until it gets cold . . . but the great fun is to approach slyly those persons whose candy appears to be well-pulled and snatch it from them. This produces great hilarity, and for the first time since I have been in Texas, this party made me think of Christmas . . . at home."[17]

8

THE OTHER FARMERS

Not all the people who settled in the West as farmers were white families from the eastern half of America. In the 1850s, families from Germany, Scandinavia and Czecho-slovakia migrated to the Great Plains region, settling in Kansas, Nebraska, the Dakotas, and Texas. A few even pushed farther west to Colorado, California, and the Northwest. The late 1800s and early 1900s brought new kinds of pioneers to the Far West—blacks from the South, Chinese, Japanese, and Filipinos.

A few blacks, mainly women, came west as slaves attached to the wagon trains of their white masters. Biddy Mason and her three daughters walked behind the huge, 300-wagon train of her master, driving a flock of sheep. And we know of at least one black woman who made the journey alone. A white woman named Margaret Frink noted in her diary that she saw a black woman on the trail "tramping along through the heat and dust, carrying a cast iron bake stove on her head, with her provisions and a blanket

Blacks were also part of pioneer movement to the West.

piled on top . . . bravely pushing on for California."[1] Was she an escaped slave making a break for freedom or a freed slave striking out on her own?

While slavery as an institution was outlawed in most of the Far West, blacks were not necessarily welcomed. Oregon, for example, had laws restricting blacks from settling. Still, blacks who had come as slaves were usually able to gain their freedom. A slave known only as "Mary" was brought to San Jose, California, in 1846 by her master. When she learned that Mexican law prohibited slavery, she sued for her freedom and became the first western slave to win her liberty through the legal system. Robbin and Polly Holmes and their children were brought to Oregon as slaves in 1844 by a master who promised them freedom in return for helping him start a farm. When he tried to keep their children, the Holmeses sued and won them away from him.[2]

Most blacks who migrated west made their way to towns and cities. But a few became homesteaders. In 1910, a black businessman named Oliver T. Jackson and his wife, Minerva Mattlock Jackson, founded an all-black farming community near Greeley, Colorado. The inhabitants called it "Dearfield" because the land was "so dear to us." The Jacksons' dream was to enable black people to become self-sufficient farmers and merchants. In the early years, the men in the community worked out of town, often for the railroads, while the women did the farming. Sarah Fountain, a teacher in Dearfield in 1918, explained:

"Every household expected the woman in the home to do the work. A woman works everywhere, she worked in the home, would put her cooking on before she went to the field, and then came back and tended to it, serve it, and, if necessary, go back out to the fields, or milk the cows, she would do that. . . . That was a hardship area, you had to irrigate from windmills, with all that blowing sand. They'd come from fertile lands, better farms, but they went there to stick it out."[3]

Several women homesteaded alone in Dearfield, among them Olietta Moore's mother and aunt. "Mother was widowed and homesteaded 160 acres in Dearfield so that Grandpa would have a place to garden and putter around on. They worked in the fields, raised corn; they would bring it to Denver and give it away to friends."[4]

Dearfield grew into a thriving farm community of 700 that lasted into the 1930s. It failed, finally, because of low market prices and a severe drought. "It all dried up and blew away," said one former Dearfield resident.[5]

THE TOWN OF
DEARFIELD
WELD COUNTY

A Valley Resort

DEARFIELD LODGE

DEARFIELD LUNCH ROOM

NOW that we have the best of accommodations here, the next thing is "Where shall we go for a little recreation and a good country lunch or dinner?"

FILLING STATION

Oliver T. Jackson (inset, with unidentified child) was a black farming homesteader. He and his wife, Minerva, founded the black community of Dearfield, Colorado, in 1910. The poster shown here was designed to encourage blacks to come to Dearfield.

Chinese immigrants came to this country in the 1860s. By 1870, there were 63,000 Chinese in America, 77 percent of them in California, though Chinese settled in Idaho and Montana as well. Most Chinese immigrants came to do manual labor in the gold mines and on the railroads. They also helped to drain California's swamplands for farming.

Many Chinese laborers who were digging ditches for white farmers had been fruit farmers themselves in China. They taught their employers how to plant and cultivate their orchards. But the Chinese farmworkers wanted to farm their own land instead of working for others. Some became tenant farmers—they would use the white landowners' land and equipment to raise fruits and vegetables and then share the profits with them.

Nevertheless, most Chinese farm laborers continued to work long, hard hours for white landowners. They were paid $30 a month, which was $10 or $20 less than white workers. The Chinese men could live cheaply because they had left their families back home in China, but most of them never made enough money to send for their families.

The Chinese farmworkers made a huge contribution to California's economy. In 1893, a California newspaper wrote, "The Chinese . . . are expert pickers and packers of fruit. It is difficult to see how our annual fruit crop could be harvested and prepared for market without the Chinaman."[6] Chinese farmers also experimented with new methods of farming, and it was a Chinese farmer in Oregon named Ah Bing who first cultivated the delicious cherry of that name.

In spite of all this, many Californians distrusted and feared the Chinese for no other reason than because they looked different from other Americans and came from a foreign land. These people lumped the newly arrived Chinese with the newly freed blacks and believed both were a threat to the white race. They referred to the Chinese as "nagurs," and a magazine cartoon of the time showed the Chinese as bloodsucking vampires with dark skin and slanted eyes.[7] White farm laborers even burned the fields

Chinese farm workers curing raisins in California in 1890

and farms of landowners who employed Chinese workers. In 1882, responding to anti-Chinese feeling, the U.S. Congress passed the Exclusion Act, which banned Chinese from immigrating for ten years.

By the late 1880s, Japanese immigrants had begun to replace the Chinese in farmwork. They worked in the Vaca Valley of California, on farms near Tacoma, Washington, and in the beet fields of Idaho, Colorado, and Utah. Like the Chinese, the Japanese, too, had been farmers in Japan and were not satisfied with working for others.

Sakitaro Takei described how he got started in 1908 in the Yakima Valley by leasing land from Indians. "Fortunately, probably because they were also suppressed by the whites as colored people, the Indians were very friendly toward Japanese and glad to lease their land." He went on to describe how he survived: "The house was a tent-house with apple-boxes for tables and chairs. I took a bath with water heated in a tub. As for green vegetables, I picked wild grass called 'Jimmy Hill mustard' . . . it grew alongside the tracks and out of it I made hot salad, boiled greens and pickles. I worked like a horse or a cow; I went to the fields before dawn and came back when it got too dark to see. The truth is I worked about eighteen hours a day with no recreation—nothing—simply work."[8]

Another Japanese farmer expressed her feelings about farming in the Yakima Valley in a short poem, called a tanka:

> Yakima Valley
> And the springtime wind raging . . .
> Dust from field and road,
> Sand from desert, sifting in,
> The entire house full of it.

The main obstacle to farming the fertile soil of Washington and Oregon was the need to clear the land of trees and sagebrush. This was usually done by using teams of oxen or horses to yank the tree stumps out of the ground. Even as late as 1908, Japanese farmers who settled in Washington's Yakima Valley remembered doing this work more or less by hand. Sakitaro Takei recalled, "Empty-handed we began clearing the land. . . . First we knocked down the clumps of sagebrush with a mattock [a kind of hoe] and, piling them up, we set fire to them. As it was troublesome to dig them out one by one, I shaved them down with a long iron rail pulled by eight horses. This horse-drawn rail mowed them down very easily, just like shaving your beard with a razor. Sage, which has shallow roots, was easy to wipe out. . . . In this way I cleared five acres and grew cantaloupe, tomatoes and onions."[9]

The Japanese were so successful at farming that, for example, by 1910, they were producing 70 percent of California's strawberries. One of the reasons for their success was the *kenjinkai*, cooperative associations that Japanese farmers formed for mutual support. Through the *kenjinkai*, Japanese farm families could get together for social activities like picnics and festivals. More importantly, farmers could get loans and share valuable information about agricultural techniques. As one Japanese farmer explained to his son, "If you hold *hashi* [chopsticks] individually, you can certainly break them all, but if you put them together, why you can't break a bunch of *hashi*. And so, like that, as a family we should stick together, but also as a community we should be sticking together."[10]

But like the Chinese before them, Japanese farmers soon became the victims of racial prejudice. Some Californians began to fear that too many Japanese were coming to this country, and that they were "taking over" farming in their state. A California senator campaigned for office on the slogan, "Keep California White." (Japanese farmers responded by saying, "Keep California green.")

In 1913, California passed a new law forbidding the Japanese from owning land, which was meant to discourage Japanese immigrants from coming to America. Japanese farmers felt angry and betrayed that their hard work and contributions to California's economy were not valued. Some Japanese farmers got around the law by putting their land in the names of their American-born children. But in the early 1920s, the Alien Land Law was passed and amended, which made it illegal for "aliens" to "acquire, possess, enjoy, use, cultivate, occupy or transfer real property." Because of the Alien Land Law, one Japanese farmer remembered, "there were many who changed their occupations, swallowing their tears."[11]

THE CHANGING
FRONTIER

Although settlers continued to stream into the West from all directions, there came a time when the frontier could be said to be closed. By 1890, so many people had settled in the West that the U.S. Census Bureau announced the end of a frontier line.

But other important events also marked the end of an era. The settlement of the West could not have happened until the "Indian problem" had been resolved. From the 1850s into the 1870s, the Indian wars raged. Indian tribes found their hunting grounds crowded with white settlers. The buffalo they had always depended on for survival were being slaughtered by the thousands by white bounty hunters. The Indians were desperate and fought back fiercely. Thousands of Indians were massacred by the army, and, in return, Indians attacked and massacred white settlers.

Mary Geisel Blake was thirteen in 1856 when her family was attacked in the night by Indians near Elizabethtown, Oregon: "Mother . . . ran out to help Father. The Indians were trying to kill Father with their knives. Mother grabbed at one of the Indians. She caught his knife, but the Indian pulled the knife out of her hand and the sharp blade nearly severed her little finger. One of the Indians held her while the others finished killing Father. The Indians took Mother and me outdoors and tied us and then went back and killed my three brothers. John was nine years old, Henry seven, and Andrew five."

The Indians took Mary, her mother, and her three-week-old sister with them on a terrifying journey to their camp, where another prisoner, a black man, bandaged her mother's finger and comforted her. For this, the Indians killed him. Mary's mother and sister were traded to white settlers, but the Indians felt they had been cheated and Mary had to spend one more night alone in the Indian camp. "As I slept that night all alone in an Indian tepee, my dreams were filled with dread, for I was only 13, all alone in a camp of hostiles who were planning to kill all settlers in the coast country."[1] Mary survived the night and was set free by the Indians the next day.

Most homesteaders felt they had a right to take land belonging to the Indians. But Phoebe Judson, who settled in Oregon Territory in 1853, showed an unusual sympathy for the Indians on whose land she had settled. "How could they realize they were trespassing our rights, when no doubt this spring had been one of their favorite camping grounds and hunting places . . . for generations? The earth with its haunts, and trails, had been as free for them to roam, hunt, and fish as the air they breathe, and we, in reality, were the interlopers."[2]

Still, by the end of the 1870s almost all Indian tribes had been driven onto reservations. George Manypenny, a

The Flathead Indian reservation in Montana around 1900

commissioner of Indian affairs who negotiated with the Indians, wrote: "By alternate persuasion and force some of these tribes have been removed, step by step, from mountain to valley, and from river to plain, until they have been pushed halfway across the continent. They can go no further; on the ground they now occupy the crisis must be met, and their future determined."[3]

The completion of the transcontinental railroad and new lands opened up by Congress in the 1870s brought even more farmers into the plains regions that had been dominated by cattle ranchers. Farmers saw the cattlemen as outlaws overrunning their pastures with destructive cattle. They put up barbed wire fences that blocked trails and kept cattle from all-important water holes. This infuriated the ranchers, who called farmers "hay shovelers," "plow chasers," and "nesters." Farmers and ranchers battled fiercely over water rights and land. Ranchers believed farming would destroy the West and mean the end of cattle ranching as they knew it.

But what really dealt the killing blow to open-range ranching was the catastrophic weather of 1886–1887. First came a summer of record-breaking heat and low rainfall. Water holes and streams dried up, and the grass withered. Soon many of the cattle were thin and in a weakened condition. The first snowfall of the year came early, in November, and from then on until spring, deep snow blanketed the western ranges from the Dakotas to Texas. The cattle were unable to get down to the grass, and when the temperatures plunged to -68°F, thousands of cattle were killed by the cold. "When the spring finally arrived," wrote one historian, "cattlemen witnessed a sight they would

Feed could be hard to find when snow covered the range.

never forget. In every ravine there was carcass piled upon carcass, dead steers along the fences, and trees stripped of their bark."[4]

This disaster changed cattle ranching forever. Few ranching operations, large or small, survived the winter. Ranchers who did survive had to do things differently. They had to keep their herds down to manageable size, grow their own hay to feed them in winter, and begin to fence their lands. Now cowboys spent their time mending fences instead of riding the range. The last of the great cattle drives from Texas to Kansas took place in 1896. An old cowboy named Teddy Blue lamented, "Riding fences and rounding up pastures ain't anything like the way we used to work cattle in the days of the open range."[5]

Just as many ranchers had been defeated by nature, some farmers were driven back east by the harsh winters, droughts, and grasshopper plagues that destroyed their crops in the 1890s. But new farmers kept coming, their journey made easier by the network of railroads that by now crisscrossed the country. By 1910, most of the territory open to homesteading had been settled and was being farmed or ranched.

And what of the original pioneers, those restless seekers who traveled thousands of weary, perilous miles in search of richer soil and a milder climate? Many found exactly what they were looking for and stayed in the West for the rest of their lives. Here is what Mary Colby wrote to her brother and sister in Massachusetts from Oregon Territory in 1849:

> Dear Brother & Sister:
> It is a long time since we have seen each other but I have not forgotten you altho many miles of

land and water separate us. . . . I suppose you would like to hear how we like this country and how we prosper in the first of our living here. I did not like [it] very well, but after we had taken our claim and became settled once more I began to like [it] much better and the longer I live here the better I like [it]. The summer is beautiful and not hot a very little rain tho it is not so warm in the summer here as it is in the States. The nights are cool and comfortable and I can sleep like a rock. The winters is rather rainy but it is not cold and so bad getting around as it is in the States. Here the grass is fresh and green the year round and our cattle are all fat enough now for beef. There is not a month in the year but I can pick wildflowers or some strawberry blossoms.

As to our prosperity, we are getting along as well as one could expect. We have a section of land one mile square in the best part of Oregon. It is prairie all except a strip of timber on two sides of it with a stream of water running through each piece of timber. Our stock consists of seven cows, one yoke of oxen, six calves, fifteen hogs and 24 hens. . . . I think with good health and good economy we shall get along very well. I cannot say that I wish to go back to the States to live at present if ever. I know when one gets comfortably fixed here they can live as well as they can with half the labor that you do in the States . . . we live in a dry cabin, it has two rooms and is very comfortable . . . so I am content with it till we can have a better one . . . give my love to all your children and please to accept a good share yourself . . . .

Yours,
Mary M. Colby [6]

SOURCE NOTES

1. LEAVING HOME

1. John Mack Faragher, *Women and Men on the Overland Trail* (New Haven, Conn.: Yale University Press, 1979), 17.

2. *Tsagigla'lal: She Who Watches*, Washington Women, A Centennial Celebration, vol. 1, June 1992. Compiled and written by Jennifer James Wilson and Brenda Owens-Klimek. (Olympia, Wash.: Office of Superintendent of Public Instruction, 1989), 65.

3. Lillian Schlissel, *Women's Diaries of the Westward Journey, 1840-70* (New York: Schocken, 1982), 20–21. Reprinted by permission of Schocken Books, published by Pantheon Books, a division of Random House, Inc.

4. Ibid., 28.

5. Ibid., 42–43.

6. Ibid., 77.

7. Fred Lockley, *Conversations with Pioneer Women*. Compiled and edited by Michael Helm. (Eugene, Ore.: Rainy Day Press, 1981), 283–284.

8. Dee Brown, *Gentle Tamers: Women in the Old Wild West* (Lincoln: University of Nebraska Press, 1968), 95.

9. Schlissel, *Women's Diaries*, 99.

10. Brown, *Gentle Tamers*, 101.

2. NOT A TRIP FOR THE FAINTHEARTED

1. Schlissel, *Women's Diaries*, 39.

2. Ibid., 80.

3. Ibid., 83.

4. Faragher, *Women and Men on the Overland Trail*, 89.

5. Schlissel, *Women's Diaries*, 55.

6. Ibid., 205.

7. Brown, *Gentle Tamers*, 102.

8. Schlissel, *Women's Diaries*, 204.

9. Ibid., 176.

10. Ibid., 212.

11. Ibid., 59.

12. Brown, *Gentle Tamers*, 102.

13. Schlissel, *Women's Diaries*, 175.

14. Ibid., 172.

15. Ibid., 126–127.

3. SEEING THE ELEPHANT

1. Schlissel, *Women's Diaries*, 179.

2. Ibid., 182.

3. Ibid., 180.

4. Brown, *Gentle Tamers*, 102.

5. Schlissel, *Women's Diaries*, 67.

6. Ibid., 71.

7. Ibid., 96.

8. Ibid., 226.

9. Lockley, *Conversations with Pioneer Women*, 140.

4. SETTLING IN

1. Lockley, *Conversations with Pioneer Women*, 167.

2. Schlissel, *Women's Diaries*, 53.

3. Anna Howard Shaw, *Story of a Pioneer* (New York: Harper, 1915), 120.

4. Sara McAllister Hartman. Memoirs. (expanded manuscript) University of Washington Library, Manuscripts and Archives Division.

5. Brown, *Gentle Tamers*, 192.

6. Ibid., 198.

7. Cathy Luchetti and Carol Olwell, *Women of the West* (Berkeley: Antelope Press, 1982), 167.

8. Brown, *Gentle Tamers*, 199.

9. Lockley, *Conversations with Pioneer Women*, 158.

10. Sara McAllister Hartman, Memoirs.

11. Ibid.

12. Ibid.

5. STARTING FROM SCRATCH

1. Faragher, *Women and Men on the Overland Trail*, 52.

2. Luchetti and Olwell, *Women of the West*, 166.

3. Elenore Plaisted. Papers held by author.

4. Luchetti and Olwell, *Women of the West*, 167.

5. Lockley, *Conversations with Pioneer Women*, 292.

6. Clark C. Spence, *The American West: A Source Book* (New York: Thomas Y. Crowell, 1966), 145.

7. Brown, *Gentle Tamers*, 208.

8. Joanna L. Stratton, *Pioneer Women* (New York: Simon and Schuster, 1981), 61.

6. LONGHORNS AND WOOLLIES

1. Ottilie Fuchs Goeth, *Memoirs of a Texas Pioneer Grandmother, 1805–1915* (Burnet, Tex.: Eakin Press, 1982), 45.

2. Ibid., 46.

3. Ibid., 41.

4. Joan M. Jensen, *With These Hands: Women Working on the Land* (New York: Feminist Press, 1981), 133.

5. Ibid.

6. Agnes Morley Cleaveland, *No Life for a Lady* (Lincoln: University of Nebraska Press, 1977), 110. Reprinted by permission of Houghton Mifflin Company.

7. Robert A. Bennett, *We'll All Go Home in the Spring* (Walla Walla, Wash.: Pioneer Press Books, 1984), 279.

8. Russell Freedman, *Cowboys of the Wild West* (New York: Clarion Books, 1985), 35.

9. Leonard Dinnerstein, Roger L. Nichols, and David M. Reimers, *Natives and Strangers* (New York: Oxford University Press, 1979), 209.

10. Ibid.

11. Otto Merdian, "Pioneer Ranching in Central Montana," *Frontier*, no. 3 (March 1930): 251.

12. Ibid., 247.

13. Goeth, *Memoirs of a Texas Pioneer Grandmother*, 82–83.

14. Luchetti and Olwell, *Women of the West*, 29.

15. Jensen, *With These Hands*, 133.

16. Elinore Pruitt Stewart, *Letters of a Woman Homesteader* (Boston: Houghton Mifflin, 1914), 16.

17. Ibid., 17.

18. Ibid., 134.

7. GETTING ALONG

1. Brown, *Gentle Tamers*, 195.

2. Lockley, *Conversations with Pioneer Women*, 256.

3. Eula Precious Fisher, taped interview, Washington Women's Heritage Project Oral History. Collection, University of Washington Libraries.

4. Brown, *Gentle Tamers*, 196.

5. Ibid., 201.

6. Ibid.

7. Luchetti and Olwell, *Women of the West*, 169.

8. Lockley, *Conversations with Pioneer Women*, 141.

9. Ibid., 292.

10. Faragher, *Women and Men on the Pioneer Trail*, 56.

11. Lillian Schlissel, Byrd Gibbens, and Elizabeth Hampsten, *Far from Home: Families of the Westward Journey* (New York: Schocken, 1989), 23.

12. Brown, *Gentle Tamers*, 203.

13. Jensen, *With These Hands*, 137.

14. Lockley, *Conversations with Pioneer Women*, 251.

15. Fisher, taped interview.

16. Stratton, *Pioneer Women*, 155.

17. John E. Baur, *Christmas on the American Frontier, 1800–1900* (Caldwell, Idaho: Caxton Printers, 1961), 248, 138.

8. THE OTHER FARMERS

1. Schlissel, *Women's Diaries*, 136–138.

2. William Loren Katz, *The Black West* (Garden City, N.Y.: Doubleday, 1971), 93.

3. Sue Armitage, Theresa Banfield, and Sarah Jacobus, "Black Women and Their Communities in Colorado," *Frontiers*, vol. II, no. 2, 1979, 38.

4. Ibid.

5. Ibid.

6. RuthAnne McCunn, *An Illustrated History of the Chinese in America* (San Francisco: Design Enterprises of San Francisco, 1979), 39.

7. Ronald Takaki, *Strangers from a Distant Shore* (Boston: Little, Brown, 1989), 101.

8. Kazuo Ito, *A History of the Japanese Immigrants in North America* (Seattle, Wash.: Japan Publications, 1973), 427.

9. Ibid., 429.

10. Takaki, *Strangers from a Distant Shore*, 193.

11. Ibid., 204.

9. THE CHANGING FRONTIER

1. Lockley, *Conversations with Pioneer Women*, 35–37.

2. *Tsagigla'lal*, 68.

3. Arrell Gibson, *The West in the Life of the Nation* (Lexington, Mass.: Heath, 1976), 123.

4. Sanford Wexler, *Westward Expansion: An Eyewitness History* (New York: Facts on File, 1991), 273.

5. Freedman, *Cowboys of the Wild West*, 62.

6. Schlissel, *Women's Diaries*, 156–157.

FURTHER READING

BOOKS

Aaseng, Nathan. *From Rags to Riches*. Minneapolis: Lerner, 1990.

Alter, Judith. *Growing Up in the Old West*. Chicago: Watts, 1991.

———. *Women of the Old West*. New York: Watts, 1989.

Bakeless, John, ed. *The Journals of Lewis and Clark*. New York: Penguin, 1964.

Bennett, Robert Allen. *We'll All Go Home in the Spring*. Walla Walla, Wash.: Pioneer Press, 1984.

Binns, Archie. *Peter Skene Ogden: Fur Trader*. Portland, Ore.: Binford and Mort, 1967.

Blumberg, Rhoda. *The Great American Gold Rush*. New York: Macmillan, 1989.

Brown, Dee. *Gentle Tamers: Women in the Old Wild West*. Lincoln: University of Nebraska Press, 1968.

———. *Hear That Lonesome Whistle Blow: Railroads in the West*. New York: Holt, 1977.

Carter, Harvey L. *Dear Old Kit*. Norman: University of Oklahoma Press, 1968.

Clappe, Louise (Dame Shirley). *The Shirley Letters: From the California Mines, 1850 1852.* Edited by Carl I. Wheat. New York: Knopf, 1961.

Clemens, Samuel Langhorne. *Roughing It.* New York: Holt, Rinehart and Winston, 1965.

De Nevi, Don, and Noel Moholy. *Junípero Serra.* New York: Harper and Row, 1985.

Erickson, Paul. *Daily Life in a Covered Wagon.* Washington, D.C.: Preservation Press, 1994.

Fischer, Christiane, ed. *Let Them Speak for Themselves: Women in the American West, 1849–1900.* Hamden, Conn.: Archon, 1977.

Fisher, Leonard Everett. *The Oregon Trail.* New York: Holiday, 1990.

Harte, Bret. *The Luck of Roaring Camp.* Providence, Rhode Island: Jamestown, 1976.

Hoobler, Dorothy, and Thomas Hoobler. *Treasure in the Stream: The Story of a Gold Rush Girl.* Morristown, New Jersey: Silver Burdett, 1991.

Jessett, Thomas E. *Chief Spokan Garry.* Minneapolis: T. S. Denison, 1960.

Johnson, Paul C., ed. *The California Missions.* Menlo Park, Cal.: Lane Book, 1964.

Katz, William. *The Black West.* Seattle: Open Hand, 1987.

Lapp, Rudolph. *Blacks in Gold Rush California.* New Haven: Yale University Press, 1977.

Lasky, Kathryn. *Beyond the Divide.* New York: Dell, 1986.

Levy, Jo Ann. *They Saw the Elephant.* Hamden, Conn.: Archon, 1990.

Lewis, Oscar. *Sutter's Fort: Gateway to the Gold Fields.* New York: Knopf, 1976.

Luchetti, Cathy, and Carol Olwell. *Women of the West.* Berkeley: Antelope Island Press, 1982.

McNeer, May. *The California Gold Rush.* New York: Random House, 1987.

Meltzer, Milton. *The Chinese Americans: A History in Their Own Words*. New York: HarperCollins, 1980.

Morris, Juddi. *The Harvey Girls: The Women Who Civilized the West*. New York: Walker, 1994.

Moynihan, Ruth B., Susan Armitage, and Christiane Fischer Duchamp, eds. *So Much to Be Done: Women Settlers on the Mining and Ranching Frontier*. Lincoln: University of Nebraska Press, 1990.

Nabakov, Peter. *Native American Testimony: An Anthology of Indian and White Relations, First Encounter to Dispossession*. New York: HarperCollins, 1972.

Rappaport, Doreen, ed. *American Women: Their Lives in Their Words*. New York: HarperCollins, 1992.

Ray, Delia. *Gold, the Klondike Adventure*. New York: Lodestar, 1989.

Schlissel, Lillian. *Women's Diaries of the Westward Journey*. New York: Shocken, 1982.

Smith, Carter. *Bridging the Continent: A Sourcebook on the American West*. Brookfield, Conn.: Millbrook Press, 1992.

Steber, Rick. *Grandpa's Stories*. Prineville, Ore.: Bonanza, 1991.

Stewart, George R. *The Pioneers Go West*. New York: Random House, 1987.

Stratton, Joanna. *Pioneer Women*. New York: Simon and Schuster, 1982.

The Trailblazers. *The Old West*. New York: Time-Life Books, 1979.

Tunis, Edwin. *Frontier Living*. New York: HarperCollins, 1976.

Van Steenwyk, Elizabeth. *The California Gold Rush: West with the Forty-niners*. Chicago: Watts, 1991.

Watt, James W. *Journal of Mule Train Packing in Eastern Washington in the 1860s*. Fairfield, Wash.: Ye Galleon Press, 1978.

Weis, Norman D. *Helldorados, Ghosts and Camps of the Old Southwest.* Caldwell, Idaho: Caxton Printers, 1977.

Wilder, Laura Ingalls. *West from Home.* New York: HarperCollins, 1974.

Wilson, Elinor. *Jim Beckwourth: Black Mountain Man and War Chief of the Crows.* Norman: University of Oklahoma Press, 1972.

Young, Alida O. *Land of the Iron Dragon.* New York: Doubleday, 1978.

TAPES AND COMPUTER SOFTWARE

American West: Myth and Reality, Clear View, CD-ROM.

Dare, Bluff, or Die, Software Tool Works, CD-ROM, DOS.

Miner's Cave, MECC, Apple II.

Morrow, Honere. *On to Oregon!* Recorded Books, Inc., Prince Frederick, Md. Three cassettes.

Murphy's Minerals, MECC, Apple II.

Oregon Trail II, CD-ROM, Windows.

The Oregon Trail, MECC, Apple II, MS-DOS, 1990.

Santa Fe Trail (Educational Activities).

Steber, Rick. *Grandpa's Stories.* Bonanza. Cassette.

Wagons West, Focus Media, 485 South Broadway, Suite 12, Hicksville, New York, 11801.

INDEX